A Family in Chile

A pronunciation guide for the Spanish names
and words used in this book appears on page 28.

LIBRARY OF CONGRESS CATALOGING-IN-PUBLICATION DATA

St. John, Jetty.
   A family in Chile.

   Summary: Presents the life of an eleven-year-old boy
and his family in central Chile, describing his school and
recreational activities and the work of his father.
   1. Chile — Social life and customs — Juvenile literature.
2. Children — Chile — Juvenile literature. [1. Family life —
Chile. 2. Chile — Social life and customs] I. Araneda, José
Armando, ill. II. Title.
F3060.S7 1986   983'.0647   85-23987
ISBN 0-8225-1667-5 (lib. bdg.)

Manufactured in the United States of America

    4   5   6   7   8   9   10   95   94   93   92

A Family in Chile

Jetty St. John

Photographs by José Armando Araneda

Lerner Publications Company · Minneapolis

Tonino Fuentes, 11, lives in the countryside of Chile, not far from Santiago, Chile's capital. On a clear day, he can see the snow on the Andes mountains.

Chile is a long, thin strip of land lying between high mountains on the east and the Pacific Ocean on the west. The northern part of the country is desert and contains many valuable minerals, such as copper, iron ore, and gold. The southern part of the country reaches down to the tip of South America.

SOUTH

CHILE

Lo Barnechea
Valparaiso
Santiago

Pacific Ocean

Andes Mountains

PERU

BRAZIL

ARGENTINA

Cape Horn

AMERICA

Like Tonino and his family, most of the people in Chile live in the central part. There the climate is pleasant and the soil is fertile.

Almost five hundred years ago, Spanish conquerors, or *conquistadores*, came to Chile in search of gold. When they arrived, they found Incas and Mapuches (also called Araucanians) living there. The Spaniards defeated these native people and took their riches and much of their land. The land was divided into large estates run by the Spaniards.

Tonino and his family live on a farm, or *fundo*, in a *comuna* in the Las Condes valley. A *comuna* is a region similar to a county. The land is hilly with scattered trees and a stream running through it. In the summer the grass gets dry and brown. The *fundo* is owned by a wealthy man of Spanish descent, whose family has owned it for generations.

Don Luis is Tonino's father. He is a *huaso*, or horse trainer. He trains young stallions, which are kept in a stable on the *fundo*. The stallions belong to a friend of the land owner. They will be ridden in a rodeo when they have been taught what to do.

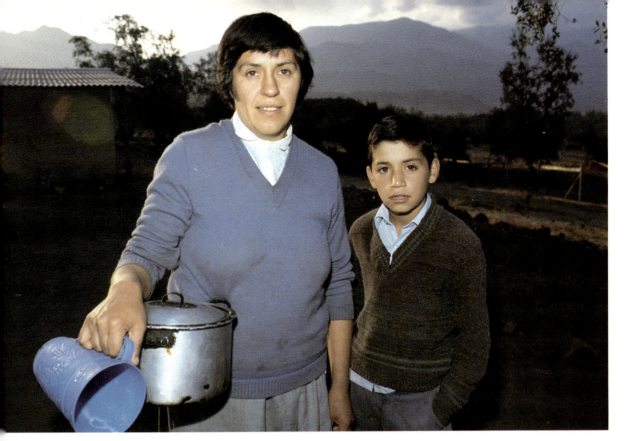

Everyday at sunrise Tonino and his mother go down to the barnyard to milk their two cows. One by one, Tonino catches each cow and ties her back legs together. A calf gets the first drink, and then Tonino's mother fills up a jug for breakfast.

At 9:00 A.M., the family has breakfast. Paulina, who is 14, makes *cafe con leche* with the fresh milk. She also serves homemade rolls.

Often while the family is eating breakfast, Tonino's *abuelo*, or grandfather, arrives. Señor Fuentes brings the day's supply of drinking water with him.

Sometimes Alejandro, Tonino's little brother, spends the night with his *abuelo*. Then he rides home with him in the morning.

Señor Fuentes is Don Luis's father. He lives near a stream about three miles (5 kilometers) from Tonino's family. He grows grapes and is also a skilled rider. He owns many horses which live on the *fundo*.

After breakfast, Don Luis goes out to the stables to work with the horses. This chestnut-colored stallion is Talamar. Don Luis has been preparing him for the rodeo.

Don Luis is also giving Tonino riding lessons. Boys may begin entering rodeos at 10 years old. Tonino is old enough to ride in a rodeo, but he still needs more practice.

First Tonino must catch Petete, his pony. He swings his lasso over his head and throws it toward the pony. He catches Petete on the second try.

Tonino then places the bridle on Petete. On young horses, a soft piece of rope is used in the mouth instead of a metal bit. By the time a horse is ready for the rodeo, he will wear a metal bit.

As Don Luis watches, Tonino gallops Petete, remembering to sit up straight in the saddle. Then Don Luis rides and Tonino follows, copying his father's moves. The riders round up a cow, and Don Luis shows Tonino how to control it with the chest of the horse.

Meanwhile, Alejandro and his mother prepare to go to the market. Paulina stays home to take care of Carolina, the *guagua*, or baby.

Once a month, Señora Fuentes takes the bus to a store near Santiago to buy dry foods and other supplies. When she returns home, the children meet her at the bus to help carry the bags to the house.

The rest of the time, she shops in the nearby village of Lo Barnechea. The stalls at the market offer the many kinds of fruits and vegetables grown in central Chile.

One stall sells fresh fish, shipped by truck from Valparaíso, the largest port city in Chile. Alejandro and his mother buy *machas*, which are a kind of shellfish.

Sometimes Tonino goes to Lo Barnechea alone to buy horseshoes or nails for his father.

On Sundays, the whole family goes to the Catholic church in Lo Barnechea. The church is on the village square. During the week, people sit on stone seats near the church and talk while their children play.

After church, Tonino's aunt and cousins often come to visit. They live in Santiago and enjoy spending a day on the *fundo*. Señora Fuentes usually makes salad, *humitas*, a sweet corn dish, and *cazuela*, chicken stew. For dessert, they have fresh melon.

The best *choclo*, or corn, for *humitas* is called *diente de caballo*, or "horse's teeth." The kernels are large. This dish has been handed down from the Mapuche Indians, who lived in Chile before the Spaniards came.

Carolina helps her mother and sister peel off the husks. The husks are saved and formed into little containers to be stuffed.

Next, the corn must be removed from the cob and mashed. Señora Fuentes adds a fried onion to the mixture, spoons it into the husks, and ties each *humita* into a little package.

The *humitas* are lowered into a pot of boiling water and cooked until the husks turn yellow. They are then ready to eat.

To make *cazuela*, To-
nino's mother fries pieces
of chicken. She then cuts
up fresh vegetables to add
to the stew.

After their Sunday meal, the children play. Tonino's older brother Luis and his cousins build a boat out of Legos, which they bought in Santiago. Paulina reads the paper, and Tonino plays his recorder.

Alejandro and his older cousin go riding. Alejandro rides La Reina, who is expecting a foal.

Every other day, Señora Fuentes makes *pan amasado*, or rolls. On Sundays, there are usually lots of people around to help her. They knead the dough and form it into small oval balls. Although they have a gas stove in the house, they bake the rolls in a special outdoor clay oven called a *horno de barro*.

Don Luis made the *horno de barro* himself. First he built the platform, and then he covered it with a thick layer of clay made from a special kind of dirt and water. In the center, he made a large pile of sticks, horse manure, and anything else that would burn. Over that, he put another thick layer of clay and cut two square openings in the mound. When the clay dried, Don Luis set the inside on fire. The fire baked the clay and made the walls and sides of the oven strong. All that was left inside were a few ashes.

Chile's summer begins in December and lasts through March. During that time, Tonino and his brothers and sisters are on vacation. School begins again in March.

Every afternoon Tonino and Luis go to school from 2:00 P.M. to 6:00 P.M. The school is five miles (about 8 kilometers) away. A *micro*, or small bus, picks them up and brings them home again. It is an all-boys school, and Tonino and his classmates must wear gray pants, a white shirt, and a blue tie.

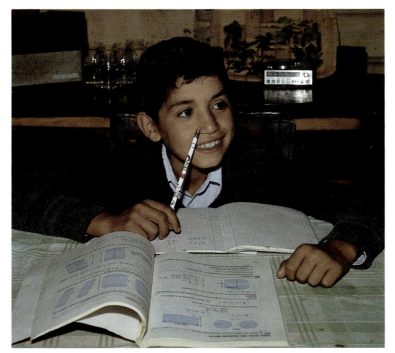

Tonino's favorite subject in school is Castilian, the Spanish language. He loves to read stories.

Tonino's class has an hour and a half of homework every day. Tonino usually does his in the morning. Then in the evening, he plays soccer. In the winter, the family plays dominoes.

Sometimes Tonino's class goes to Santiago. This year
they visited San Cristóbal, a large hill overlooking Santiago.
They got to ride a cable car to the top. Standing up there,
Tonino and his classmates were able to look out over the city.

The skyscrapers are easy to recognize from the top of San Cristóbal, but some of the older buildings are hard to pick out because they are built low to withstand earthquakes. They also saw the Mapocho River. The water in the river is cold because it has come down from the mountains.

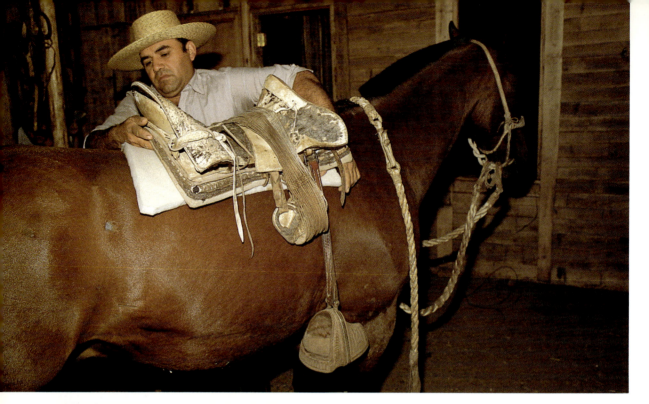

The horses keep Don Luis busy. Their hooves require cleaning, and sometimes he must re-shoe them. Often there is a saddle or bridle to make or mend.

Don Luis and Tonino wear special *apero de huaso*, or riding apparel, including riding boots and chaps. They use two kinds of saddles, one for everyday training and the other during rodeos. The rodeo saddles have hand-carved stirrups, and the reins are made from braided leather.

Don Luis has built a rodeo ring so that he and Tonino can practice with the horses.

The ring is divided into two parts. A calf waits in a corral in one side while two riders get ready. As soon as the calf is let out into the other side of the ring, the *huasos* steer her toward a padded fence. The first rider then tries to stop the calf against the fence, using the horse's chest.

If the calf is pinned by the hind quarters, the rider scores four points. If it is pinned by the stomach, the rider scores three points, and if by the shoulders, two points. No points are scored for the head. The riders take turns trying to pin the calf, and each has three tries.

Tonino's skill is improving and he will soon be ready to enter a rodeo. Then it will be time to teach Alejandro to be a *huaso*.

Spanish Words in This Book

abuelo   ah BWAY loh
Alejandro   ah lay HAN droh
apero de huaso   ah PAY roh day oo AH soh
cafe con leche   kah FAY con LAY che
Carolina   kah roh LEE nah
cazuela   kah SWAY lah
Chile   CHEE lay
choclo   CHOH kloh
comuna   koh MOO nah
conquistadores   kohn keest ah DOH rays
diente de caballo   dee EN tay day kah BAI yoh
Don Luis   dohn lu EES
Fuentes   FWEN tays
fundo   FOON doh
guagua   goo ah goo ah
horno de barro   ORN oh day BAR roh
huaso   oo AH soh
humitas   oo MEE tahs
La Reina   lah ray EE nah
Lo Barnechea   loh bar nay CHAY ah
Luis   lu EES
machas   MAH chas
Mapocho   mah POH choh
micro   MEE kroh
pan amasado   pahn ah mah SAH doh
Paulina   pah oo LEE nah
Petete   pay TAY tay
San Cristóbal   sahn kris TOH bahl
Santiago   sahn tee AH goh
señor   say NYOR
señora   say NYOR ah
Talamar   tah lah MAR
Tonino   toh NEE noh
Valparaíso   vahl par ah EE soh

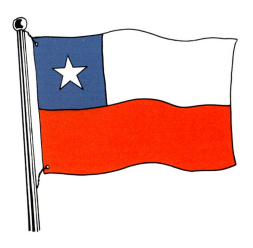

Facts about Chile

Capital: Santiago

Language: Spanish

Money: new peso

National Holiday: Independence Day, September 18

Independence Day is celebrated for two days, September 18 and 19. On this holiday, Chileans celebrate their freedom from Spanish rule, which was won in 1818. Many people dress up in brightly colored costumes and dance in the streets. There are parades everywhere.

Area: 292,257 square miles (756,945 square kilometers) including Cape Horn

Population: About 13.3 million people

Chile has less than half as many people as California

NORTH AMERICA

SOUTH AMERICA

Chile

EUROPE

A S I A

AFRICA

AUSTRALIA

31

Families the World Over

Some children in foreign countries live like you do. Others live very differently. In these books, you can meet children from all over the world. You'll learn about their games and schools, their families and friends, and what it's like to grow up in a faraway land.

Lerner Publications Company, 241 First Avenue North, Minneapolis, Minnesota 55401